EXTREME

Ocean in Motion!

Surfing and the Science of Waves

Paul Mason

A & C Black London

Produced for A & C Black by

MONKEY PUZZLE MEDIA LTD

Monkey Puzzle Media Ltd
48 York Avenue
Hove BN3 1PJ, UK

Published by A & C Black Publishers Limited
36 Soho Square, London W1D 3QY

Paperback published 2009
First published 2008
Copyright © 2008 A & C Black Publishers Limited

ISBN 978-1-4081-0029-5 (hardback)
ISBN 978-1-4081-0120-9 (paperback)

The right of Paul Mason to be identified as the author of this Work has been asserted by him in accordance with the Copyright, Designs and Patents Act 1988.

A CIP catalogue record for this book is available from the British Library.

Editor: Polly Goodman
Design: Mayer Media Ltd
Picture research: Lynda Lines
Series consultant: Jane Turner

This book is produced using paper that is made from wood grown in managed, sustainable forests. It is natural, renewable and recyclable. The logging and manufacturing processes conform to the environmental regulations of the country of origin.

Printed in China by C & C Offset Printing Co., Ltd

Picture acknowledgements
Alamy pp. 6 (Jesse Farrar), 23 (Craig Ellenwood); Sylain Cazenave p. 21; Corbis p. 20 (Clifford White); Getty Images pp. 22 (Warren Bolster), 24–25 (Sean Davey); Gary Knights p. 28; Photolibrary.com pp. 8 (Bill Brennan/Pacific Stock), 9 (Mark Gibson/Index Stock Imagery), 18 (Ron Dahlquist/Pacific Stock), 29 (Carol and Mike Werner/Phototake Science); Science Photo Library p. 7 (NOAA); Mike Searle pp. 1, 14, 15, 26; Mickey Smith pp. 16, 25 right, 27; Alex Williams pp. 4, 10, 11, 12 both, 13, 17, 19, 24 left; Darrel Wong p. 5.

The front cover shows the Hawaiian surfer Jamie Sterling at Teahupoo, Tahiti (Alamy/Surfpix).

Every effort has been made to contact copyright holders of material reproduced in this book. Any omissions will be rectified in subsequent printings if notice is given to the publishers.

CONTENTS

Abbreviations km stands for kilometres • **m** stands for metres • **ft** stands for feet • **in** stands for inches • **km/h** stands for kilometres per hour • **mph** stands for miles per hour

The biggest ride?

Imagine a wave so big that riding it is like jumping off a house, then having the house chase you down the street! That's just what happened to a lifeguard and surfer called Darrick Doerner, on 31 January 1988.

That morning, the waves at Waimea Bay in Hawaii had been just a metre high. By mid-afternoon, waves over 7 metres (23 feet) high were rolling into the bay.

The biggest **set** of the day appeared, and Doerner paddled for its biggest wave. His surfboard slid down the huge wall of water, he turned at the bottom, and rode along the wave's **shoulder**. The wave had been over 10 metres (33 feet) tall. It was the biggest wave that anyone had ever paddled their surfboard into.

Some waves are really tall. Others, like the one below, give a long ride.

set group of waves   **shoulder** part of a wave that has not yet crashed down

Surfer Laird Hamilton does a bottom turn on a 9-m (30-ft) wave in Hawaii.

Where waves come from

These gentle waves in Hawaii were made by a storm thousands of kilometres away.

The biggest wave ever ridden had travelled thousands of kilometres before it reached Waimea Bay in Hawaii. Surfing waves often travel a long way to get to the beach.

Waves are made by the wind. Strong winds send waves rippling across the surface of the sea, like a bedsheet flicked up so that air goes underneath it.

The stronger the wind, the bigger the waves it produces. The best surfing waves of all are produced by giant storms called **hurricanes**. Keen surfers learn to watch the weather carefully, hoping to see that a storm or hurricane will be sending waves their way!

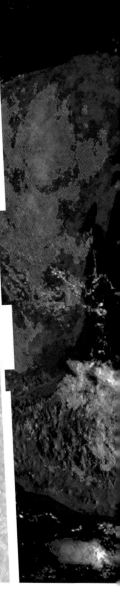

hurricanes   storms with wind speeds of at least 119 km/h (74 mph)

The biggest wave

In 1933, in the North Pacific, the crew of the *USS Ramapo* spotted the biggest wave ever seen. The wave they saw was a monster 34 metres (112 feet) high – as tall as a seven-storey building!

High winds around **eye** of storm

Wind whips up waves on surface of water.

Waves travel away from storm – and towards surfers!

eye   the centre of a storm

A satellite photo of Hurricane Dean, taken on 20 August 2007.

Friend and foe

Waves are exciting to ride, but they can also be deadly dangerous. On 26 December 2004, a giant tsunami wave hit the coasts of Southeast Asia. In some places, the tsunami was three times as tall as the biggest wave ever ridden. Nearly a quarter of a million people were killed.

Even waves much smaller than the tsunami cause damage. In fact, waves are constantly wearing away at our coastline. Some unlucky people even find their garden and house falling into the sea as a result!

The streets of Phuket, in Thailand, flooded with water from the December 2004 tsunami.

The village that fell into the sea

In 1917, the fishing village of Hallsands, in Devon, UK, was hit by a terrible storm. The waves swept through the village, wrecking it. Today, most of its buildings still lie under the ocean.

tsunami   a giant wave caused by an earthquake

*Coastal **erosion** at Sandy Bluff, California, USA. Imagine living here!*

In the next few months, these houses will fall into the ocean.

CLIFF

CLIFF

CLIFF

WAVES

WAVES

WAVES

Waves eat away at cliff, causing erosion.

erosion the wearing away of rock or soil

9

How waves break

Although waves look like moving water, for most of a wave's life it hardly moves any water at all! How is this possible?

Surfing waves are actually waves of **energy**, travelling away from the storm that caused them. These **pulses** of energy travel across the surface of the ocean. The water moves up and down as the energy passes, but is left behind in the same place. Only the energy moves on.

Surfers try to catch waves as they break. This is the moment when the wave's energy is released.

Only when the waves reach the beach do they start to move water forwards. As the wave hits shallower water, it slows down. Because the base of the wave is nearer the seabed, it is in shallower water than the top of the wave so it slows down more. The top of the wave spills over, or "breaks".

energy power, or the ability to do work   **pulses** beats, or throbs

When waves break

Waves generally break when the water beneath them is 1.3 times their own height. So a 2-metre (6.5-foot) wave breaks in water that is 2.6 metres (9 feet) deep, and so on.

ENERGY

DEEP WATER

Energy from a distant storm travels across the surface of the ocean.

As waves hit shallower water, they start to break. Water tumbles down from the top of the wave to the bottom.

SHALLOW WATER

Catching a wave

Surfers only have a split second to catch a wave as it breaks. Yet just learning to stand up on a surfboard is about as hard as standing on a log in a river, never mind catching a wave at the right time.

1. The surfer paddles hard, trying to get his board moving almost as fast as the wave.

2. As the wave pushes the board to the beach, the surfer pushes down on the deck and whips his feet up.

To make learning easier, beginner surfers look for particular kinds of wave. The best waves for learning break slowly and gently. The **peak** crumbles down the **face** instead of being thrown forwards. Because waves like this are less powerful and slower moving, beginners have more time to experiment and learn.

3. He stands up and starts to turn the board along the wave.

Surfer turns this way.

peak   the spot where wave first breaks   **face**   unbroken front of wave

Welcome to the Green Room

The "Green Room" is a surfing name for the space inside a tubing wave, like the one on the right. Most surfers never get to enter the Green Room – but that doesn't stop them trying!

Tubing waves are among the most dangerous ones to ride. They tube because they break on a steep, shallow seabed. The water in front of a wave like the one on the right might only be 1 or 2 metres (3.3 or 6.5 feet) deep. If surfers fall, or "wipe out", they can hit the seabed hard.

Oh, man!

Wipeouts on tubing waves can be very painful.

tubing wave   wave that forms a tube of air inside as it breaks   **wipeouts**   falls or crashes

Lip thrown out in front of wave.

Only the tail and **rail** of board bite into wave face.

Shallow water

Surfer makes rapid progress this way!

Surfing strummer

Musician Jack Johnson is a keen surfer. He had his front teeth knocked out at the age of 17, while surfing the famous tubing waves at Pipeline, Hawaii.

Teetering on the brink of a painful wipeout, surfer Spencer Hargraves races through the Green Room.

lip   the breaking tip of a wave   **rail**   edge of surfboard

Riding big waves

Big-wave surfers are probably the ones other surfers admire most. It takes a lot of courage to paddle your board into a wave as tall as a house!

*Big-wave surfing in Hawaii. Many big-wave spots are a long way **offshore**.*

One of the problems for big-wave surfers is that the bigger a wave is, the faster it is moving. This is because big waves break in deep water, so they are not slowed down much by a shallow bottom. It is hard to get your board moving fast enough to catch big waves.

Catching big waves is made even harder by what seems like wind. This is caused by air rushing up the wave's face.

offshore   out to sea

Gravity pulls surfer towards base of wave.

gravity   force that attracts objects to each other

Tow-in surfing

Tow-in surfing is the most revved-up kind of surfing there is! These surfers use wetbikes to give them a high-speed tow into the world's biggest waves.

Until tow-in surfing was invented, the biggest waves went unridden. These giant waves, some over 15 metres (50 feet) tall, break far out at sea. They are travelling so fast that no surfer could paddle his or her board quickly enough to catch them. Then someone realized that a tow from a wetbike would let surfers zoom along at up to 40 kilometres per hour (25 miles per hour) – fast enough to catch much bigger waves.

A wetbike tows the surfer up to speed, before he lets go of the tow line and catches the wave.

wetbikes water craft like motorbikes, but with a propeller instead of wheels

Surfer Laird Hamilton rides the wave known as "Jaws", in Maui, after a tow from a wetbike. The waves at Maui, in Hawaii, are famous around the world.

Helicopter tow-in

Some surfers have taken tow-in surfing a step further. Amazingly, they have started using helicopters to get a tow into the wave!

"Impact zone", where wave smashes down.

Tow-in surfer's feet are attached to the board with foot straps to help prevent wipeouts.

Tow-in surfboard has heavy, lead centre, to stop it taking off.

Wetbikes wait in a safe area, in case the surfer has to be rescued.

Water like concrete

Most people think of water as soft, something you can easily slide into. But if you hit water hard enough, it feels more like concrete.

When you hit the water's surface after a bad wipeout, you're travelling at high speed. The wave throws you forwards, towards the beach, and gravity pulls you down. Your body doesn't drop through the surface and under water. Instead it skids along, like a stone skimming along the surface. Only after a few spins in what surfers call the "washing machine" do you sink down and escape the wave's clutches!

Ouch!

"I came up, and something was hitting me in the back of the head. I thought, 'What's that hitting me in the back of the head?' Then I looked round, and it was my foot."
– Hawaiian surfer Titus Kinimaka describes the effects of a **REALLY** bad wipeout.

Brrgh! Ice-cold surfing

Surfing the far north

Today, there are surfers as far north as Alaska and Scandinavia. Even with the warmest wetsuit, they only manage to stay in the water for half an hour at a time!

Every year, there are more and more surfers in the water. Sometimes, the only way to escape the crowds is to surf in freezing-cold water, where few others dare to go.

Where there ARE big crowds, surfing's rules are very simple:

- The surfer nearest the peak has the right to catch the wave.
- On an unbroken wave, the first person to their feet gets the wave.
- A surfer riding in has to avoid people paddling out.

To avoid crowds like this, some surfers have begun to explore the surf in cold parts of the world such as Alaska, Iceland and Scandinavia.

Toasty!
Body heat warms trapped water inside wetsuit, keeping surfer warm.

Brrrgh! Cold water in

Hat keeps head warm.

Gloves and boots stop **extremities** getting cold.

Today, some surfers choose to avoid the crowds by going to places where the water and air are cold. This means they have to have some specialist cold-water equipment in their kit bag!

This surfer, in Ireland, is wearing a full winter surfing kit.

extremities   parts of the body that stick out from the torso, especially the hands and the feet

Ripped away

Every year, some surfers are killed in accidents. Understanding the currents caused by waves might stop you being one of the casualties.

With big surf like this on the beach, there will be lots of water trying to escape back out to sea. This causes strong, dangerous rip currents.

Waves cause movements of water called rip currents (rips), or undertows. These fast-moving flows of water can quickly drag surfers and swimmers out to sea. Rips form in places where the seabed is deeper than the bed either side of it.

currents flows of water

Fortunately, if you are a confident swimmer it's possible to escape a rip current. Keep calm. Look towards the shore to see if anyone has seen that you need help. If so, wave both arms above your head – the international signal for "HELP!"

Swim ACROSS the current. Most rips are quite narrow, and you should soon escape its clutches. Once you are out of the current, start swimming back to shore. If you find yourself back in the current, swim sideways again.

No waves break where seabed is deeper. Water escapes as a strong rip current.

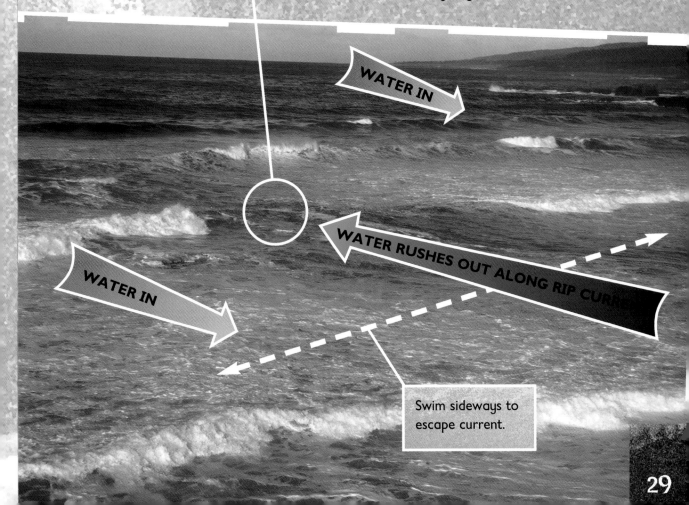

WATER IN

WATER IN

WATER RUSHES OUT ALONG RIP CURRENT

Swim sideways to escape current.

Index